ZLATEH THE GOAT

Works by Isaac Bashevis Singer:

1) *Zlateh The Goat and Other Stories* (1966)
2) *A Day of Pleasure: Stories of a Boy Growing Up in Warsaw* (1969)
3) *The Fools of Chelm and their History* (1973)
4) *Naftali the Storyteller and His Horse Sus and Other Stories* (1976)
5) *The Power of Light – Eight Stories for Hanukkah* (1980)
6) *Stories for Children* (1984)
7) *More Stories From My Father's Court* (2000)

N.B.:Details from the original works have been changed to interweave the stories.

The works are found in the various scenes as follows:

Scene 1: The Moon in a Barrel – The Snow in Chelm (1)
The Mixed Up Feet (1)
The Silly Bridegroom (1)
Moon / Telescope / Holy Books (2) (6) (7)
Scene 2: The Silly Bridegroom (1)
The Squire (5)

ZLATEH THE GOAT

*A Play in Two Acts Based on Stories by
Isaac Bashevis Singer*

ISAAC BASHEVIS SINGER

TABLE OF CONTENTS

Dramatis Personae

Reuven (RV) – furrier, stern father, very religious, wary of new ideas

Leah (LH) – Reuven's wife, an orthodox Jewish Mama

Tzipa (TZ) – oldest daughter, about 16, meekly obedient (until Scene 7) and not too bright

Aaron (AA) – 13, rebellious and full of questions

Chana (CH) – about 8, smart, used to being babied

Lemel (LM) – perhaps 20, from Chelm, an illiterate trader, simple but good-hearted

Baba Shosha (SH) – Reuven's mother, a doting and meddling grandma, uses a cane

Zlateh (ZL) – placid elderly goat

Uncle Jacob (JB) – Reuven's younger brother, about 2, university student, progressive and sometimes abrasive

TIME: 1910-1915

PLACE: Yanev, a small village in Poland

Leah and Shosha, as married women, wear long-sleeved garments and kerchiefs that conceal their hair. Reuven and Lemel have long beards and earlocks. Aaron has earlocks.

They wear long coats (gaberdines) and hats or skullcaps at all times. Uncle Jacob, more progressive, has a short clipped beard and no earlocks.

N.B.: Staging parts of the narrated stories in various ways—shadows, scrim, puppets—is discouraged. As much as possible, the audience should be engaged with the story, the storytellers, and the music.

VISUAL REFERENCES: For photos from the 1920s, see Alter Kacyzne's Poyln: Jewish Life in The Old Country *(1999).*

Vocabulary

A gute voch	"A good week" (said at the end of Sabbath)
Chelm	traditional town of fools
dreidel	gambling game with top; the top itself
Good yontif	"Happy Holiday" (generic)
groschen	(plural) coins, cents
gulden	(plural) money (like dollars or pounds)
Gute Shabbes	"Good Sabbath" greeting)
Haukkah	(literally "rededication") Jewish holiday in December, commemorating Jewish defeat of Syrians.
kishkes	guts, innards
mazel tov	good luck, congratulations
menorah	religious candlestick
Nes Gadol Haya Sham	"a great miracle happened there!" (referring to Hanukkah, letters on sides of a dreidel)
oi vey	"Oh woe" (expression of dismay)

Sabbath stewpot	no cooking is allowed on Sabbath, so families leave a pot of stew overnight in the over – at home or at the local bakery – for a hot midday meal
shammes	"sexton", the middle candle in a Hanukkah menorah, used to light others
Shechechiyanu …	"for keeping us alive", prayer for many special occasions
shlemiel	a person for whom nothing goes right
Torah	first five books of the Bible (Old Testament)
vey iz mir	"woe is me"

ACT ONE

Scene One

Music suggesting Hanukkah blessing. Lights up on main room of Aaron's family house. Woodstove, sofa, table, chairs/ Reuven's desk at SR. front door to kitchen and barn. Through windows we can see falling snow.

On the table us a Hanukkah menorah. The shammesh and first candle are lit. Around the table Aaron, Chana, Leah and Tzipa hold hands.

AA/CH/LH/TZ	… Shehechiyanu v'kiyemanu v'higiyanu lazman hazeh. Amen
LH	*reaching out to hug all* Happy Hanukkah.
CH	Mama, when is Papa coming home?
LH	Soon, I hope. Tzipa, go set the menorah in the window.
TZ	Yes, Mama. *takes menorah UP to windowsill*
AA	I guess it's good that it's so cold this winter. Papa can sell more furs.

LH	Yes, but I wish he didn't have to work so late. *takes dreidel from apron pocket* Now, would you like to play dreidel?
AA/CH/TZ	*ad lib* Yes! I will! Me! *they flock around the table*
LH	Let's start with, oh, ten groschen each. *hands out coins*
AA/CH/TZ	*ad lib* Oooh! Thank you, Mama! I go first! *Door opens. It's Reuven. Children drop game and run to greet him.*
RV	*stamping snow off boots* Good yontif. Leah, I've brought home a guest. He's just putting a blanket over his horse.

Leah glances anxiously about the room.

AA	Who is it, Papa?
RV	You go enjoy your game. *children return to table* He's a nice young man named Lemel. He buys and sells. He has his own horse and wagon. He brought some rabbit skins to my shop and we got to talking. I think he might be a good match for Tzipa.
LH	Tzipa! Go take off that apron and comb your hair.
TZ	Yes, Mama. *exits to kitchen*

LH	But Reuven, what makes you think – I mean, the boys here in Yanev tease Tzipa because she's – well, a little – simple.
RV	Yes, Leah, let's be honest, she has about as much brains as Moshe her goldfish. *Aaron and Chana giggle.* But she's sweet and obedient and you've taught her to sew and cook. Besides, Lemel isn't a village boy. He's from town.
LH	From Chelm?
RV	Yes.
LH	Ohhhh.
RV	It's worth a try, isn't it? *a knock* Come in, Lemel.
LM	*entering* How did you know it was me?!
RV	*a nod to Leah* A lucky guess? Everyone, this is Lemel. My wife, Leah. My son, Aaron. My little girl, Chana. *Tzipa enters shyly; Reuven holds her before she can escape* My older daughter, Tzipa.
LM	Good yontif.
RV	*with his arm around Tzipa* Shall I tell you a story about my girl here?
TZ	*embarrassed* Oh Papa ...
RV	One night she saw the full moon reflected in a barrel of water. She thought it had fallen in, so

she put a lid on the barrel so the moon would not escape. The next morning she said *letting Aaron and Chana join in* "I caught the moon! I caught the moon! Papa, Mama, come and see!"

LH   Of course we lifted the lid, and there was no moon. Then she cried and wanted us to call the police because someone must have stolen the moon!

LM   *seriously* Well, of course you should have called the police. The moon is even more valuable than the sun, because it shines at night when it's dark and we need the light.

Tzipa reacts. For once someone didn't laugh at her.

RV   *another nod to Leah* See?

AA   Papa, what is the moon made of?

RV   The Lord Almighty created the sun and the moon and placed them in the sky. That is all we need to know.

AA   Uncle Jacob says the moon has mountains and craters. You can see them with a telescope.

RV   So? Can you see Heaven with a telescope? What do Jacob and his university professors want to do?

	Fly to the moon and bring back a piece?
AA	Science can answer everything. I want to study science. I want to know, why is it hot in the summer and cold in the winter? How deep is the ocean?
RV	There are mysteries in the Torah that are deeper than the ocean. You should be studying holy books, not science. Compared to the wisdom of the Almighty, the whole world is one big Chelm.
LM	*defensive* People think all of us in Chelm are fools. It's not so. Of course sometimes we do foolish things, like everyone else. My Aunt Basha is always saying, "Lemel, you're a dummy, a dolt, a dunderhead –"
LH	Now, Lemel, that's enough.

Knock on the back door.

LH	Tzipa, go and let Zlateh into the house.
TZ	Yes, Mama.
LM	Zlateh?
	Tzipa opens back door. Zlateh enters – an old dignified white goat. While Leah speaks Zlateh walks slowly to her place by the stove and sits.

LH	She lives in a pen out in the shed. She knocks on the door with her horns when she wants to visit.
LM	You let a <u>goat</u> come into your house?
AA	*going to Zlateh* Zlateh is a very special goat. She saved my life in the snowstorm last year. Didn't you Zlateh?
ZL	Maaa.
AA	You see? Her whole language is just one word. But sometimes I think I know what she means. When I grow up I want to learn the language of goats.
RV	Now, Aaron – though, it is said that King Solomon talked to the beasts of the earth and the birds of the air. Aaron, you are not a fool but you are not a Solomon either.
LH	*peacemaking* Lemel, tell us about your family.
RV	*chuckling* Yes, tell them about your sisters.
LM	Oh – well – since my parents died, I and my three sisters live with Aunt Basha. She has a very small house, so I sleep in the barn and all three girls sleep in one big bed. Usually they get up very early to help Aunt Basha milk the cows and do the chores.

But one morning last week they didn't get up. Aunt Basha went into the room and found them all struggling and screaming and pulling each other's hair.

TZ What happened?

LM Well, they said, in their sleep they had gotten their feet mixed up, and now they didn't know whose feet belonged to whom, and so of course they couldn't get up.

TZ And what did Aunt Basha do?

LM She went to ask the Elders of Chelm what to do. But first she told my sisters, "Now you stay in bed and don't budge until I return. Because once you get up with the wrong feet, it will be very difficult to set things right."

The Chief Elder clutched his beard with one hand, placed the other on his forehead and thought very hard. He said, "This happened in Chelm once before, many years ago, and oh, how much trouble it was. But there is a solution. Basha, take a stick and – unexpectedly – whack the blanket where the mixed-up feet are. It is possible that in surprise and pain each girl will grab at her own feet and jump out of bed."

	She tried it, and you know what? It worked!
TZ	The Elders of Chelm must be very wise.
RV	*who has been following the interaction* Lemel, you have no parents and you are an independent businessman. So I am going to ask you: Would you like to marry my daughter?
LM	M-marry Tzipa?
RV	Who else, Chana?
LM	Oh, of course not. I mean, yes. I mean – I would be honored Reb Reuven, to accept your daughter Tzipa as my bride.
RV	Wonderful!
LH	Wonderful!
TZ	Wonderful!
ZL	Maaa.
RV	*going to his desk* All we have to do is sign your marriage contract. Then you will be engaged. I have the papers right here.

Tzipa bursts into tears.

LH	Tzipa? What is it, honey?
TZ	Mama, how can I marry a total stranger?
LH	Everyone does it.

RV	The parents always arrange these things. You have to trust that we know what's best for you.
LH	After the wedding, the husband and wife become close and are no longer strangers. I married a stranger, too.
TZ	No, Mama. You married Papa. How can you make me marry a complete stranger?
RV	Look, sweetheart – you and Lemel sign the marriage contract. The moment you sign it, Lemel becomes your betrothed. And when you marry, you will not be marrying a stranger. You will be marrying your betrothed.
TZ	*comforted* Oh. All right.
LM	I'm sorry, Reb Reuven. I can't sign the contract.
RV	What? Why not? What's the matter?
LM	I never learned to write my name.
RV	*relieved* All right, here – you sign with three dashes. *Lemel does* And Tzipa, you sign with three circles. *Tzipa does* There! It's a match. Mazel tov!
ALL	Mazel tov!
ZL	Maaa.
RV	Lemel, you are my future son-in-law and it's the first night of

	Hanukkah. So I would like to give you a little gift –
LM	A pocket knife! With a pearl handle. Thank you, Reb Reuven. That's a very nice gift.
LH	Now you get along home. Don't make your Aunt Basha worry about you.
LM	All right. *it's sinking in* Thank you – good yontif – good night – I'm going to get married.
TZ	I'm going to get married!
AA/CH	Tzipa's going to get married!
ZL	Maaa.

END SCENE ONE

SCENE TWO

Music. The second candle is lit. Aaron, Chana and Tzipa at table playing dreidel. Reuven at his desk, glasses on, reading. Zlateh is by the stove. Leah enters from kitchen.

LH	Well, who's winning?
AA	Chana. She's cleaning us out.
RV	You should give some of your money to the poor. Charity is a great deed.
LH	Now, Reuven, don't start preaching to them. It's Hanukkah. It's the only holiday of the year when they can play.
CH	*looking at dreidel* "Nes gadol haya sham." Papa – why doesn't God work miracles now, in our time?
RV	*pulling at his beard* Who says He doesn't? God works miracles in all generations. Some people think there were more miracles in ancient times. Well, that's not

13

	true. The truth is, miracles are rare in all times. If too many miracles happened, people would rely on them too much.
LH	That's right. God wants us to do things, to make an effort, not to be lazy. By the way, Tzipa, I need your help in the kitchen.

A knock at the front door.

TZ	Oh Mama, that might be Lemel.

Reuven opens the door. Lemel enters.

LM	*fuddled as usual* Rev Reuven – goof yontif everyone – I was about to go back to Chelm but I remembered, Aunt Basha said to tell you she heard that your brother Jacob may be coming from Warsaw to visit you.
RV/LH	Jacob!
AA/CH/TZ	*all together* Uncle Jacob!
LM	*babbling, looking at Tzipa* Well, she heard it from Feyvel the butcher who heard it from a peasant whose wife goes to the doctor who has a nephew in Warsaw and …
RV	*not happy* After a year and a half at that university he finally comes to

	see his only brother. Maybe miracles <u>do</u> happen.
LH	Lemel, what did Basha say about your nice pocket knife?
LM	*abashed* She didn't see it. I lost it.
LH	Lost it?
LM	I'm sorry. I tried to be careful. I put it in the wagon with the hay, but when I got home I couldn't find it. maybe it fell through a crack. Oh, Aunt Basha is right, I'm a dummy, a dolt, a dunderhead –
RV	*kindly* Stop that, Lemel. A knife you don't put in a load of hay. You should have put it in your pocket.
LM	You're right, Reb Reuven. I'll know what to do next time.
LH	Tzipa, why don't you give Lemel some of our fresh eggs to take home? I know that'll please Basha.
TZ	Yes, Mama. *dashes into the kitchen*
AA	*who has been pondering* Papa, was it a miracle when Zlateh saved my life?
ZL	Maa.
RV	Well – perhaps it was more than a coincidence.
LM	What happened to Zlateh and Aaron?
RV	Well, it's a long story – you need to get home –

Tzipa enters with exaggerated care.

TZ	Here are the eggs, Lemel. *sets them on table and Lemel picks them up*
LM	Thank you. Uh, thank you, good yontif, good night. exit
LH	Tzipa, come with me. we need to talk
TZ	Yes, Mama. *Leah and Tzipa exit to kitchen*
RV	Of course, there are some cases where only a miracle could save someone.
CH	*spotting a lead-in* A story! Tell us the story, Papa.
AA	Don't stop the game. I want to win back what I lost.
RV	You can play again tomorrow. This is a story about a Hanukkah miracle that happened right here.
CH	Really?!
AA	All right.
RV	This happened when your grandfather was a little boy. The village of Yanev was much smaller then than it is today. Where we are sitting now there was a pasture for cows.
CH/AA	Really?!
RV	There was a tailor in the village named Falik. He had a wife, Sarah,

and three children. One year the family had a lot of bad luck. Their tailor shop burned down. Then Sarah became very ill. The village healer came with leeches and cups but nothing helped. Sarah died.

Then Falik himself became sick. He couldn't even get out of bed, and so he couldn't work. All the village people tried to help the family, sending them bread and cheese and meat, but Falik wouldn't accept charity. The oldest boy, Mannes, sold all the silver plates and spoons and pieces in the house, until there was nothing left but a beautiful antique Hanukkah menorah from Sarah's family. Mannes wanted to sell that, too, but Falik said, "Wait until after Hanukkah."

Hanukah came, and there was a lot of snow, frost, blizzards. The children brought the menorah to Falik's bed so he could light it and say the blessing, and they set it in the window. Then they sat at the table. Imagine, one year before, they were playing dreidel and eating pancakes with jam. This year Sarah was gone and their father was sick. They had nothing to eat. The house was cold.

Suddenly, someone knocked at the door!

AA Who was it?

RV That's what the children said to each other. Who could it be? Mannes said, "It's probably some-one with charity. Papa said not to accept any gifts." He didn't want to answer the door. But the knocking went on and on. Finally Mannes went to the door.

When he opened it, he saw a squire –

CH A what?

RV A nobleman. He was tall and broad-shouldered, in a long fur coat – not just squirrel or muskrat but black sable – all the way to his ankles, and a fur hat sprinkled with snow. A squire could own a whole village and be as rich and mighty as a king. And squires didn't usually visit poor Jewish families at night.

AA What did he want?

RV The squire said to Mannes, "I was passing in my sleigh and I saw the silver lamp in your window. I never saw anything like it in my life before. The lion, the eagle, the flowers! Is this some Jewish holiday? Where are your parents? Why do you light just one light when there are eight holders?

AA

RV

What did Mannes say?

Well, he knew how to speak to an important man. He said, "Come in, your excellency. We are honored by your presence."

The squire came in and stared at the menorah. Mannes and his sisters told him the story of Hanukkah, the Jewish victory over the Syrians and the miracle of the lamp that burned for eight days. Then the squire saw a dreidel on the table and said, "And what is that?" Manned explained the game to him.

The squire asked, "Could I play dreidel with you? My driver will wait for me."

Of course the three children had no money to play with. The squire said, "Never mind. I want to buy that beautiful silver lamp, but I don't have enough money with me, so I'll give you an advance." And he threw a big bag of gold coins on the table.

The children were so astounded that they forgot their hunger. The game began, and anyone could see it was a wonder from heaven. The children kept winning and he squire kept losing. In one hour the squire lost all his gold.

AA   Wasn't he angry?

RV   No. he just laughed and said, "Lost is lost. My driver and my horses must be cold. Good night, happy Hanukkah and don't worry about your father."

The squire left, and the children just stared at the pile of gold coins on the table. The little ones started crying. Mannes ran to the door, but the squire, his driver, the sleigh and the horses had all vanished. There was no sound of sleigh bells. There were no tracks in the snow.

Then they heard Falik, their father, calling. He had been nearly dead, but the moment the squire left, Falik woke up a healthy man. Nothing but a miracle could have saved him.

CH   *after a pause* Who was the squire?

RV   Who knows? The prophet Elijah? He certainly was no Polish squire.

AA   Did he ever come back for the menorah?

RV	Not that anyone knows. Of course some people in the village say it was just some rich spendthrift who was in a mood to squander his money. But it has been said, when God works a miracle, He often does it so that it looks like a natural event. Isn't it still a miracle?

Leah and Tzipa enter with plates of pancakes.

LH	Why are you all so quiet? Is the game over?
CH	I want to give some of my Hanukkah money to a poor tailor.
LH	Reuven? Were you preaching to them?
RV	I didn't preach. I just told them a story.

*** END SCENE TWO ***

SCENE THREE

Music. The third candle is lit. Tzipa and Leah at table sewing. Zlateh offstage. Chana wrapped in a blanket, lying on sofa. Aaron is sitting on floor, showing her something in a book. Reuven at his desk.

Sharp rap on the door with a cane. Then door flung open. The tranquil scene is shattered by the arrival of Baba Shosha. Wrapped in a shawl, leaning on a cane, kerchief askew, a basket on her arm. She is everything you love – and resent – in a grandmother.

SH	Happy Hanukkah, everyone!
AA/CH	Baba Shosha!
RV	Mama!
SH	*bustling to each one* Reuven! And how's my little Chanele? A little sick, I heard? No, no, you stay there and rest. Aaron! Now you're a grown man, can up still give your grandma a kiss?
AA	Good yontif, Baba Shosha.
SH	And Tzipa! Just think of it, my granddaughter getting married.

	I was so excited when I heard. She looks thin, Leah, are you feeding her enough?
LH	If you had seen her eating pan-cakes last night, you wouldn't worry. Good yontif, Shosha.
SH	Well, I brought just the thing to put some roses in those cheeks. *sets basket on table, brings out a crock* Some of my strawberry jam.
TZ/AA/CH	*ad lib* Jam! Thank you, Baba Shosha. Can we have some now, Mama?
SH	*another packet* And here's some herb tea for Chana's throat. Be sure you let it steep at least ten minutes. She'll be as good as new.
LH	Now Shosha –

A tap at the back door.

LH	Tzipa, go and let Zlateh in.
TZ	Yes, Mama.

Tzipa goes to back door. Zlateh enters and comes to place by stove. Aaron comes to pet her.

SH	You still let that goat come right into your house?
LH	*with some defiance* Zlateh is old and it's cold out in her pen. After what

she did for Aaron, she's always welcome in my house. She's always well-behaved and she never tries to give me advice. *takes tea and exits to kitchen*

Baba Shosha and Zlateh eye each other

ZL   Maaa.

SH   *to Reuven* If only your brother Jacob would arrive. Then we'd have the whole family together under one roof again.

RV   When he comes, he comes. I can't tell him anything. You can't tell him anything. He couldn't stay here in Yanev and go into business like a sensible man. No, he had to run away to Warsaw and study Science! He believes anything they tell him – professors! Zionists! Socialists!

SH   He's a grown man, Reuven, he's not your little brother now. You don't have to wipe his nose for him –

Knock at the front door. Leah reenters. Reuven opens the door.

LM   Good evening, everyone – Reb Reuven – Leah – Tzipa – *with formal importance* Reb Reuven, Aunt Basha invites you and your family to come spend Sabbath with us in Chelm tomorrow. She wants to meet my, um, my betrothed and the in-laws. And you can meet her and my sisters. *more boyish* Please come. I can drive you in the wagon and bring you back after sundown Saturday.

LH   A whole day in Chelm?

RV   Tell Basha that we would be honored to spend Sabbath with you. Well, come in, Lemel, don't let all the heat out. *Lemel enters, closes door* Lemel, this is my mother, Shosha, Tzipa's grandmother.

SH   Lemel! What's that all over your coat?

LM   I'm sorry. I tried to be careful. When I drove home yesterday, the road was full of holes and rocks, and I bumped against the side of the wagon and the eggs got broken.

RV   You put the eggs in your pocket?

LM   Didn't you tell me to?

RV   *shaking his head* A knife you put in your pocket. You should put eggs in a basket with some straw and a rag on top so they don't break.

LM   You're right, Reb Reuven. I'll know what to do next time.

Chana starts to cough.

LH	Lemel, since you didn't get to use those eggs, why don't we give you one of our chickens?
SH	Good idea. He can't break a chicken!
LH	Tzipa, go to the shed with Lemel and give him a nice chicken.
TZ	Yes, Mama. It's this way, Lemel.
LM	Thank you, Leah. That's a very nice gift. Well – I'll see you tomorrow –

Chana's cough gets worse.

SH	Leah, you can't take that sick child on a long wagon ride in the cold.
LH	For once I agree with you. But –
AA	*after a moment* Mama, why can't Chana and I stay here? I can take care of her.
LH	Are you sure? What if she gets worse?
CH	I'm all right, Mama.
AA	Please, Mama. I'll take out Sabbath stewpot to the baker's oven. And I'll feed the chickens and I'll milk Zlateh. It's only one day.
LH	Reuven?

RV	Aaron, do you promise to stay right here and take care of Chana?
AA	Yes, Papa.
SH	And if there's anything you can't handle, you come and get me, won't you dear?
AA	Yes.
RV	All right. Lemel, Tzipa and Leah and I will come and visit you tomorrow.
LM	Wonderful! I'll come and get you with the wagon an hour before sundown.
TZ	*shyly* It's this way, Lemel.

Lemel and Tzipa exit by back door. After a duel of glances with Bava Shosha and Reuven, Leah follows.

ZL	Maaa.
SH	*bustling again* Well, I must get back to the house. Jacob could be arriving any time –
CH	*sitting up* Baba Shosha, van you tell us a story?
SH	Isn't it time for you children to go to bed?
CH	Please, just one story?
AA	A scary one?
SH	All right.
	Once there was a family with eight children, four boys and four girls. The boys all had earlocks and the

girls all had braids. One Hanukah they were all playing dreidel and they forgot about bedtime. Mother and father reminded them that it was getting late. But the children who were winning wanted to win more, and those who were losing wanted to win back what they had lost.

music

Suddenly there was a knock at the door. In came a young man with a curled mustache, high boots, a coat lined with fox fur and a hat with a feather in it. He was covered with snow but he looked merry and untroubled. He had lost his way in the blizzard, he said. Could he stay 'til morning? The boys unharnessed the horses from his sleigh, took them in the stable and fed them. Mother asked the guest if he were hungry. "Like a wolf," he replied. Would he join them in playing dreidel? "Gladly," he said, and sat down at the table.

faster music

He ate pancakes, drank tea and puffed smoke rings form his pipe.

He bet silver coins and lost them. He put out gold coins and lost them, too. He lost and laughed, lost again and joked. Midnight passed and bedtime was forgotten.

music becomes surreal

Then the oldest boy asked, "what's wring with out animals?" The dogs were barking, the hens cackled, geese honked, the horses neighed and stamped their hooves. The boy looked at the wall and noticed there were only eight shadows instead of nine. The stranger did not cast a shadow.

Now, everyone knows that demons cast no shadows. When the clock struck thirteen, there was no doubt who their guest really was.

grotesque music

The demon rose with a loud laugh, stuck his tongue out to his belly and grew twice as tall. Horns came from behind his ears. He began to spin like a dreidel, round and round – plates clattered to the floor and the house shook like a ship on a stormy sea. Mice and goblins appeared and whirled around in a ring, laughing and screaming. Suddenly, the demon sprouted wings, clapped them together and crowed – "Cock-a-doddle-do" – and they all disappeared. All the demon's money vanished, too.

> Gold and silver turned to dust
> In the snow a track of rust
> Gone the treasure on the bench
> Nothing left but the devil's stench
> Elflocks in the children's hair
> Devil's dirt was everywhere.
> Good the devil's gone away
> With his horses and his sleigh
> Such a pity, such a shame
> Hanukkah night and a devil's game.

Leah and Tzipa reenter.

LH	Shosha! They're going to have nightmares again.
CH	You forgot the ending?
SH	The ending?
CH	Yes. Where did the demon fly off to?
SH	Oh yes. *music* He flew off beyond the Mountains of Darkness,

beyond the Castle of Asmodeus, to the wilderness near Mount Seir, where no people walk and no cattle stray, where the earth is iron and the sky is copper.

AA   Tell us another one!

SH   No, I have to go home. And you have to go to bed, or some kind of Demon will be after you. There will be another night and another story.

*** END SCENE THREE***

SCENE FOUR

Music. The fourth candle is lit. Chana and Aaron are both reading. Zlateh offstage. Chana is restless.

CH	When will Mama and Papa be back?
AA	They won't even leave Chelm until after sunset tomorrow. The horse gets to rest on Sabbath, too.
CH	I wish I could study Hebrew and Talmud and Gemara like you.
AA	Our religious school is only for boys. But you can read the scripture in Yiddish. That's why they publish the special book for women.
CH	I don't want to grow up to be a woman. I don't want to marry some stranger and change my name and shave off my hair and wear a kerchief. And have a mother-in-law order me around like Baba Shosha does to Mama.

AA	Well, that's not for a long time yet. Maybe you could go to a university with me. Uncle Jacob said there are girls in Warsaw who study law and medicine and painting and everything.
CH	Are you going to study science?
AA	I don't know. Maybe I'll study writing. Stories are magic. I'd like to tell stories and publish books.
CH	Tell me a story, Aaron. A new story, one <u>you</u> made up.
AA	Well, I started thinking about this one. It's called "Into The Wild Forest."
	Once there was a boy named Haiml. His mother died, and his father remarried to a wicked woman. The stepmother was so mean to Haiml that he ran away and went to live in the wild forest. He found a hollow tree, a thousand-year-old oak, and he lived there.
CH	What did he eat?
AA	Berries and mushrooms and plants, whatever he could find. One night he heard a moaning sound, like a girl crying, way down in the tree. This hollow tree was actually the entrance to an underground cave where a monster

named Mordush lived. Mordush had kidnapped a girl, Rebecca, and wanted to force her to be his wife. Rebecca was the daughter of a wealthy merchant, and she was already engaged to, un, Ben Zion, the rabbi's son. Of course she didn't want to trade him for this old monster with one eye in the middle of his forehead. Besides, Mordush ate people, and he wanted Rebecca to eat people too.

CH   Eeeww! So did Haiml rescue her?

AA   *sheepishly* I don't know. That's as far as I got. Even if Haiml rescued her, he couldn't marry her.

CH   Unless, maybe, Ben Zion became a hermit, or forgot her and married someone else.

AA   But Rebecca was a lot older than Haiml anyway. And maybe her rich father wouldn't approve of the match.

CH   It must be hard to write stories.

AA   Well, I'm just starting to –

A knock at the front door. Chana and Aaron look at each other.

CH   Who's that?

AA	It's not Zlateh. She always knocks at the back door. *more knocking*
CH	It's not Baba Shosha. She always knocks with her cane.
AA	Maybe it's a rich squire. But we can't play dreidel with him. We can't touch money on the Sabbath.
CH	Maybe it's a demon! *hides her head*
Voice off	Aaron! Chana! Are you awake?
CH	Oh no! It knows our names!
AA	Oh Chana! It's Uncle Jacob!

Aaron opens the door. Jacob enters – a young man with a short jacket, no earlocks, closely trimmed beard.

JB	Good yontif, Aaron! Gute Shabbes. Goodness, you're almost a man now. Chana. Mama wanted me to look in on you.
CH	Uncle Jacob! You cut your beard!
JB	Of course. No one wears long beards or earlocks or gaberdines at the University. You think I want to look like a villager? *a beat*
AA	*teasing* Cahan thought you were a demon.
CH	Mama and Papa will be glad to see you.
AA	But – Papa calls you a heretic.

JB	Well, which is worse, a demon or a heretic? Now, tell me – Tzipa's really getting marries? Who is this Lemel? What's he like?
AA	Well – he's a perfect match for her.
CH	First Papa gave him a pocket knife and he lost it. Then we gave him some eggs and he put them in his pocket and they broke.
JB	In his pocket?!
AA	Then we gave him a chicken, and he put it in a basket with a rag on top, and it smothered to death.
JB	They probably had chicken soup tonight.
CH	Papa said, "Eggs you put in a basket. You should put a chicken in a cage and give it some corn."
AA	And then Tzipa said, "You are my betrothed, so I am going to give you my dearest possession, Moshe."
JB	Moshe?
AA	Her little goldfish.
JB	What do you suppose he'll do with that? *a beat*
AA	Can I get you a cup of tea? The kettle's still hot.
JB	No thank you, Aaron. I just stopped by a for a moment – to give you these!
AA/CH	Chocolate!

JB	And – these!
CH	Storybooks!
AA	*sounding it out* Sher-lock Hol-mes.
JB	Yes, they just published him in Yiddish. The scientific detective!
AA	*dubiously* Papa says the Bible has plenty of stores. He doesn't want me to read secular books. *a beat* But I do anyway.
JB	How can you get a true education from just religious school? You're both smart, you should read everything you can. I got these books from Naftali, the peddler. He sells books off a wagon, every kind of book you can think of. Poetry, histories, novels. Storybooks are very cheap, just a few groschen.
CH	Where do all the stories come from?
JB	Some of them are very old, like the ones you heard from your Baba Shosha. And some are true stories. Almost every day something amazing happens somewhere, and people write it down. And there are writers who make up stories.
AA	They make them up? Does that mean they are liars?
JB	They are not liars. If a thing doesn't happen today, it might

happen tomorrow, or a year from now, or a hundred days from now. If not here, in another country or maybe another world. Sometimes I read a story and I say, "That's unbelievable" – but later I find out that the thing actually happened. Did you ever read about giants? When the circus came to Warsaw, I saw a giant seven feet tall, and a troupe of midgets, and horses and bears that dance to music!

AA   What's it like in Warsaw?

JB   Well – it's noisy. On my street I hear taverns and restaurants and sewing machines and peddlers yelling. You can hear radios and gramophones all hours of the day. And telephones. *Aaron and Chana react* The streets are paved with cobblestones and they're full of wagons and buggies and trolleys and electric street cars and even some automobiles. You have to be careful or a cart will knock you over.

CH   I want to go there.

AA   I want to go everywhere in the world.

JB   Well, wait until Sabbath is over, all right? I'll see you in a couple of days.

AA	Gute Shabbes, Uncle Jacob.
CH	*sleepily* Why doesn't Naftali bring his book wagon to Yanev?
JB	*leaving* He doesn't even come to Chelm. It doesn't pay. Most of the country people can't afford even a couple of groschen for story books.
AA	What do the children do without any story books?
JB	*struggling* They have to make do. Story books aren't bread. You can live without them.
AA	I couldn't live without them.

Lights fade.

*** END SCENE FOUR ***

ACT TWO

Scene Five

Music. The fifth candle is lit. Chana and Aaron are sweeping up broken jam crock.

CH/AA   *ad lib* It was your fault. No, you pushed me into the table. We have to clean it up before they get hoe. Why do I have to help, <u>you</u> broke it. You're clumsy, you're always breaking things. Look out, here they come.

Enter Reuven, Leah, Tzipa and Lemel. Tzipa is withdrawn, staying away from Lemel. Chana exits to kitchen with pieces in the nick of time.

AA   Papa! Mama! Welcome home! How was Sabbath? Hi Lemel.

They hang up coats. Lemel tries to take Tzipa's; she turns away.

CH   *reentering* What was it like at Aunt Basha's house?

LH	*with a hug* Well, you certainly look better! Basha's house is very small. Tzipa had to sleep with Lemel's sisters.
AA	*to Tzipa* Are you sure you came home with your own feet?

Tzipa looks at her feet, manages a smile.

CH	Lemel, how's Moshe?
LM	Moshe?
CH	The goldfish Tzipa gave you. *Tzipa is looking daggers at Lemel*
LM	I'm sorry. I tried to be careful. I put it in a cage and gave it some corn, but when we got home it was dead.
TZ	You murdered my Moshe!
LM	But I did what you told me! Oh, Aunt Basha is right, I'm a dummy, a dolt, a dunderhead –
RV	Lemel! I know you mean well, but you can't use yesterday's solution for today's problem. Now, I have an idea. You have your horse and wagon. You buy and sell. Why don't you make a trip to Warsaw?
LM	*astonished* Warsaw!
RV	*getting pouch from a nook at desk* Because I trust you, I'm going to give you an advance on your dowry

	as Tzipa's husband. Two hundred gulden.
LM	*awed* Two hun– ?
RV	You go to Warsaw and look for a bargain. Buy something that you can get there very cheap and that everyone needs here.
LM	All right. Thank you, Reb Reuven. That's a good idea.
LH	Stop here on your way tomorrow. We'll give you some food to take on the trip.
LM	Thank you, Leah. Good night, everyone. Tzipa – *Tzipa won't respond, even when Leah nudges her* A gute voch. *Exit*
LH	*looking at table* What happened to Shosha's jam crock?
CH	Well, I – we –
AA	*hastily* Where did you and Papa stay in Chelm?
RV	We stayed with Aunt Basha's neighbors, Mr. and Mrs. Shlemiel.
LH	*laughing, distracted* There are many Shlemiels in the world, but there must be the very first ones. Basha told us all about them.
RV	Can you believe it? Mrs. Shlemiel sells vegetables in the market, and Mr. Shlemiel stays home and takes care of the baby.

LH	And they have a rooster that lives right in the house with them.
AA	In the house!
RV	Well, I guess that's no stranger than having a goat in the house.
LH	We have to tell you the story Basha told us.
RV	One day about a week ago, Mrs. Shlemiel was going to market. She had just made a big pot of jam for Hanukkah, and she knows Mr. Shlemiel has a sweet tooth. Once he tasted the jam, he wouldn't stop eating until the pot was empty. So she said –
LH	Now, honey, there are important things I want you to remember while I'm gone.
RV	Yes – ?
LH	First, make sure that the baby does not fall out of his cradle.
RV	Good. I will.
LH	Second, don't let the rooster get out of the house.
RV	Good. I won't.
LH	Third, there is a potful of poison on the shelf. Be careful not to eat it or you will die.
RV	I – *an alarmed grunt* As soon as Mrs. Shlemiel left foe market,

Mr. Shlemiel began to rock the cradle and sing:

music

> I am a big Shlemiel
> You are a little Shlemiel
> When you grow up
> You will be a big Shlemiel
> And I will be an old Shlemiel
> When you have children
> You will be a papa Shlemiel
> And I will be a grandpa Shlemiel

LH The baby fell asleep, and Mr. Shlemiel dozed off, too. He dreamed he was the king of a distant country. He was so rich he could eat pancakes with jam every day of the year. Mrs. Shlemiel was his queen and say next to him on a golden throne. She didn't have to go to market any more.

RV Between them they shared a huge pancake spread with jam. He ate from one side –

LH – and she from the other –

RV – until their mouths met. *Kiss*

LH But then the rooster crowed. "Cock-a-doodle-do!" It had such a strong voice, it rang like a bell. Mr. Shlemiel woke up and thought the fire bell was ringing.

RV   He jumped up so fast he overturned the cradle. The baby fell out and bumped his head. Mr. Shlemiel ran to the window and opened it to see where the fire was. But the moment he opened the window –

LH   – the rooster flew out and hopped away.

RV   Hey, Rooster! You come back. Oi vey, Mrs. Shlemiel will rave and rant and I will never hear the end of it.

LH   Meanwhile the baby was crying – "Waaaahh" – he had a big lump on his forehead from the fall. When Mr. Shlemiel saw there was no fire, he closed the window, went back and comforted the baby, set the cradle back up and put him back in it.

RV   *music*

> In my dream I was a rich Shlemiel
> But awake I am a poor Shlemiel
> In my dream I ate pancakes with jam
> Awake I chew bread and onion
> In my dream I was Shlemiel the King
> But awake I'm just Shlemiel

LH   The baby finally went to sleep, and Mr. Shlemiel began to worry.

RV   When Mrs. Shlemiel comes home and finds the rooster gone and the baby with a bump on his head, she will be angrier than ever before. She'll scream and scold and call me names. She has a very loud voice. What is the sense of such a life? I'd rather be dead.

LH   So Mr. Shlemiel decided to end his life. But how to do it? then he remembered the pot of poison on the shelf.

RV   That's what I'll do. I'll poison myself. When I'm dead, she can scream at me as much as she likes. I won't hear her.

LH   He climbed up on a stool and took down the pot and began to eat.

RV   Oh, this poison is sweet.

LH   He licked the pot clean. Then he lay down on the bed. He was sure he would die soon. After an hour or two his stomach began to ache.

RV   It's not really so bad to die. With poison like this, I wouldn't mind dying every day. *yawns*

LH   He dreamed again he was a king with three crowns on his head. Mrs. Shlemiel sat next to him, looked at him lovingly and said

	shrill Shlemiel, why didn't you light the lamp?
RV	*waking* It sounds like my wife. But how can that be? I happen to be dead. Or is it possible I am still alive?
LH	It was evening. Mrs. Shlemiel lit the lamp. Then she began to scream – "Just look at the baby! He has a bump on his head! Vey iz mir! Where is the rooster? Shlemiel, what have you done?"
RV	Don't scream at me. I'm about to die. You will soon be a widow.
LH	Die? Widow? What are you talking about?
RV	I've poisoned myself. I ate your whole potful of poison.
LH	Poison? Oh you fool. That was my pot of jam for Hanukkah.
RV	But you told me it was poison.
LH	I didn't want you to eat it before the holiday. Oi vey! *starts to cry* All my jam!
RV	Oi vey! *weeping happily* I haven't been poisoned! I'm still alive! What joy!
LH	Mrs. Shlemiel was crying.
RV	Mr. Shlemiel was crying.
LH	They woke up the baby and he began to yowl, too. The neighbors

	came running, and everyone in Chelm knows the story.
AA	What happened to the rooster?
RV	It got cold and hungry wandering around outside and came home by itself.
LH	Are you sure Tzipa should live in a town with neighbors like that?
RV	Think of it this way. Compared to the Shlemiels, Lemel and his family have the wisdom of the Prophets.
CH	Did they have no jam for Hanukkah?
LH	Oh, Basha took pity on them and gave them some of hers. By the way, what happened to the crock of jam Shosha gave us?
CH/AA	Well –

*** END SCENE FIVE ***

Scene Six

Music. The sixth candle is lit. Shosha, Leah and Tzipa are at table sewing. Jacob is on sofa sharing a book with Aaron and Chana.

Reuven at his desk. He gets up, wipes frost from window and looks out.

RV   What a snowstorm! Well, for a furrier bad weather is good business.

TZ   I hope Lemel is all right on the road.

LH   You really miss him, don't you? I'm sure he's fine.

SH   He's probably sitting by the fire in an inn eating a big bowl of noodle soup.

JB   *to Aaron and Chana* Look at the snow. Did you know every flake is a little jewel with six sides, with fancy little designs and decorations? And each one is different from all the others.

CH	Why is each flake so beautiful? All it does is melt into water or people step on it.
RV	The Almighty creates everything and bestows beauty on all His creations.
AA	Oh Papa, you have the same answer for every question.
RV	The Almighty creates all wonders –
JB	*overlapping* It all comes from Nature. Science tells us that the earth was torn away from the sun and the sun's energy created the first life.
RV	*smugly* So? And Who created the sun?
JB	bringing Chana and Aaron to window Look at the frost trees on the window. Every winter they are the same. Nature has a pattern for everything. They look like fig trees and date trees.
RV	Such trees don't grow here in Poland, but in the Holy Land. The Temple in Jerusalem was destroyed because Jews sinned. But if we repent, the Messiah will come and we'll all go back to the Holy and. All the generations will live again. the light of the sin will be seven times brighter. The Temple will be

	rebuilt, and all people will live in peace.
JB	You and your stories! Why should we wait for the Messiah? We can go to the Holy Land now.
RV	That's what your Zionist friends say.
JB	Yes. But I'm not sure I agree. We need to work for a better society right here. No one should be ashamed to be poor or a worker. If the workers would unite –
RV	And how will you build this better society? By throwing bombs at the Tsar?
SH	Sha! Always the same arguments. *puts down sewing* Jacob, we'd better go home while we can still see the road.
AA	Can you tell us a story, Baba Shosha?
CH	One about a demon?
JB	Hmph! Have you read the newspapers lately? Who needs stories about demons when man himself is a demon?
SH	A demon. I can do better than that. A Hanukkah story – with the Devil himself – and the Devil's wife – and the Devil's goat.

As if on cue, a knock at the back door.

TZ	*giggling* Zlateh must have heard you. *lets Zlateh in as before*
JB	Aaron, when am I going to hear the story about you and this goat?
AA	I'll tell you before you leave, Uncle Jacob. Go on, Baba Shosha.
SH	It was a cold snowy night, like this one. The snow had been falling for three days and three nights. The wind whistled in the chimneys. *music* The Devil's wife came riding on her hoop, with a broom in one hand and a rope in the other. Behind her strode the Devil with his cobweb face, holes instead of eyes, hair to his shoulders and legs as long as stilts. In front of her ran a white goat with a black beard and twisted horns.
ZL	Maaa.
SH	In a one-room hut sat a poor boy named David, alone with his baby brother. It was the first night of Hanukkah. His mother and father had gone to the village three days earlier, when the snow began, and had not returned.

David was so worried he couldn't stay at home any longer. He lit the first Hanukkah candle, and tucked the baby in its cradle. Then he put on his quilted coat and his hat with earflaps – just like yours, Aaron – and went out to look for his parents.

This was what the Devil had been waiting for. He whipped up the storm. Black clouds covered the sky. The falling snow was dry as salt, and the air was filled with dusty white whirlwinds like goblins dancing in the cold. David could hardly see in the darkness. The wind almost blew him off the ground. He heard noises like the laughter of a thousand imps.

David realized the Devil was after him. He tried to turn and go home, but he could not find his way. The snow and the darkness swallowed everything. The devils must have caught his mother and father. Would they get him, too?

But heaven and earth have vowed that the powers of evil can never succeed completely. Even the Devil will make mistakes, especially on Hanukkah. The darkness hid the stars, but it could not extinguish the one Hanukkah candle.

David saw the candle and ran toward it. The Devil ran after him on his stilt legs, The Devil's wife followed on her hoop, yelling and waving her broom and trying to lasso him with her rope. David ran even faster. He got to his hut just ahead of the Devil. He ran in and slammed the door. In the rush, the Devil's tail got stuck in the door.

Now, what would you do if you caught the Devil by the tail?

TZ   I don't know.

CH   I'd tickle him.

AA   I'd get an ax and chop it off!

SH   That's what David said. "I've got an ax and I'm going to chop off your tail."

The Devil screamed and whimpered, "Give me back my tail."

David said, "Give me back my mother and father."

The Devil swore he knew nothing about them. David said, "I know you lie. You kidnapped them."

The Devil cried, "Have pity on me. I have only one tail." And he said to his wife, "Go bring back that man and woman we got three days ago."

The Devil's wife rode away on her hoop. Soon she returned, with David's father riding on the hoop and holding her hair. David's mother rode on the Devil's goat, grasping its black beard tightly.

David looked through the keyhole and saw his parents were really there. He wanted to open the door at once, but he also wanted to teach the Devil a lesson. So he took the Hanukkah candle and singed the Devil's tail. *sound effects* – "*tsssss… Aoooww!*"

"Now, Devil, remember – don't make trouble on Hanukkah."

Then David opened the door. The Devil licked his singed tail. *music* And the Devil, the Devil's wife and the Devil's goat ran far away, beyond the Mountains of Darkness, beyond the Castle of Asmodeus, to the wilderness near Mount Seir, where no people walk and no cattle stray, where the earth is iron and the sky is copper. *nodding to the familiar words* Let's get going, Mama. *good night.*

JB

*** END SCENE SIX ***

Scene Seven

Music. The seventh candle is lit. Aaron and Chana are at table drawing. Zlateh by stove. Reuven at desk. Tzipa pacing, uneasy.

TZ   I thought Lemel would be back by now.

RV   You really care about him, don't you?

TZ   *simply* He is my betrothed.

LH   *entering from kitchen* Be patient, honey. You know it takes a whole day to drive from here to Warsaw,

RV   I hope he didn't have an accident.
Tzipa moans

LH   Don't talk like that, Reuven. I'm sure he'll –

A knock at the front door.

TZ   *flying to door* Lemel! Lemel!

LM   *entering* Tzipa! I missed you! I came as fast as I could.

	In their shyness all they can do is touch hands
RV	*closing door behind* Lemel Come on in, future son-in-law. How was your trip to Warsaw.
LM	clutching his snow-sprinkled hat Oh, Reb Reuven, Leah, Tzipa, it was a great success. I have something here *patting his pocket* that will make us all rich.
TZ	Wonderful!
LH	Wonderful!
ZL	Maaa.
RV	Oh, don't mind her. Tell us, Lemel.
LM	Well, yesterday when I got to Warsaw I was very hungry –
LH	Tzipa, didn't you give him a chicken to eat on the road?
LM	Yes, Leah, she did. But when I opened the parcel it was raw chicken.
TZ	*bewildered* You said to give him a chicken. You didn't say anything about cooking it.
LH	Never mind, Tzipa, it's all right. Go on, Lemel.
LM	In Warsaw I came to an inn and sat down at the table. The innkeeper said, "What do you want to eat?" I said, "I'm very hungry. Bring me

everything you have and I'll eat until I'm full."

So first I had a glass of wine and some chopped liver. Then he brought me a bowl of noodle soup. He asked, "Are you still hungry?" I said, "Yes, I'm still hungry." Then I had a huge plate of meat and cabbage and potatoes and carrots. But I was still hungry. Then he brought me some fruit, and some tea and sponge cake. He asked, "Are you full yet?" I said, "It's all very nice, but I'm still hungry."

Then he brought me a cookie and said, "Try this."

I ate the cookie – and then I was full. I said, "This is amazing. If I had known you could get full by eating a cookie, I wouldn't have had to order all that other food."

I took out my money and paid for the meal. Then I thought, there isn't much food in Chelm, especially in the winter. Many people are hungry there, and in the villages. Everyone needs cookies like this.

So I asked the innkeeper, "If I pay you one hundred gulden –"

RV   Don't tell me. you paid a hundred gulden for one cookie?

LM   Of course not. Do you think I'm a fool? *a beat* I asked the innkeeper, "Would you sell me the recipe for these cookies?" He argued for a long time, but he finally sold me the recipe for a hundred gulden. *taking out piece of paper* Now Tzipa can bake cookies and I can sell them, no one will every be hungry again and we will be rich!

RV   Let me see that – *taking paper* just a moment, I need my glasses – there, now I can read. *looking it over* Oh no, Lemel, you've been swindled!

TZ   What?

LM   What? But he was such a nice man –

RV   Listen to this:

music "Take three quarts of duck's milk, five pounds of flour from iron, two pounds of cheese made from snow and half a pound of feathers from a red cow. Throw it all in a pot made of wax and let it cook three days and three nights over the fire of a potato tree. Cut out the cookies with a knife made of butter, and bake them in an over made of ice until they turn red, brown and yellow. Then dig a pit, throw in the whole mess and put a sign over it reading "Az a nar geyt in mark, rreye zikh di kremer. When a fool goes to market, the merchants rejoice."

All	*in various tones* Oh Lemel!
RV	The thief! The cheater! May his bones rot. A fire in his kishkes!
LM	I'm sorry, Reb Reuven. Oh, Aunt Basha is right, I'm a dummy, a dolt, a dunderhead –
LH	Lemel! Done id sone.
LM	It's my fault because I don't know how to read. Reb Reuven, nay I have your glasses?
RV	What? How will they help you?
LM	You put on your glasses and said, "There! Now I can read." I want to be able to read.
RV	I wish it were that easy. No, Lemel, if you want to learn to read, you'll have to go away to school and study. It takes, oh, six months, maybe a year.
TZ	*suddenly assertive* No!
LH	Tzipa!
TZ	I won't let him go away for months and months. *boldly, to Reuven* He can drive his horse and wagon and do business without reading.

RV	Don't you want him to improve himself?
LM	*side by side with Tzipa* Reb Reuven, when I went to Warsaw, I was thinking of Tzipa all the time. When I'm away from her even one day I feel like I will die of longing. If I have to go away for school for six months, I'll have to die – maybe a hundred times or more.
TZ	When Lemel is away from me even an hour, I feel like I will go crazy. So if he goes away, he will come back dead, and find me crazy, and that wouldn't be so good for either of us.
LH	Tzipa! *change of tone* I think she's right, Reuven.
ZL	Maaa.
RV	One day they are children and the next – yes, I think you should get married and stay here in Yanev.
TZ	Not in Chelm?
RV	And sleep in Aunt Basha's barn? No, you can stay in your own room. And Lemel, if you want to learn the fur business – I think Aaron wants to study something else – farther away. Maybe in Warsaw. Or even Berlin.
AA	*awed* Papa –

RV   I think you, too, can't use yesterday's solution for today's problem.

LM   I'm sorry I lost your money, Reb Reuven.

RV   Not my money, your money. It's your dowry. Besides, the innkeeper was the real fool. it is said, he who causes his neighbor to feel shame, loses Paradise himself. You and Tzipa don't have money like the squires, or wisdom like the sages, but you have more love than all of them.

*** END SCENE SEVEN ***

Scene Eight

*M*usic. The eighth and final candle is lit. Reuven at desk. Leah and Shosha at table. Zlateh by the stove. Aaron, Chana and Tzipa on sofa. Lemel stands behind Tzipa. Jacob in armchair, holding forth.

JB   … and he told me, in New York the houses go up to the sky. They have so many electric lights that night is as bright as day. they eat white bread in the middle of the week. The trains run over the rooftops and underneath the ground.

SH   *snorts in contempt* Crazy stories!

RV   But you know what happens to Jews in America. The men shave off their beards. The married women don't cover their hair. The children go to public school. They travel on the Sabbath and eat non-Kosher food. Even their rabbis are the same. They ignore the Holy Books and preach Spinoza. Oi vey,

	there are more omens every day. It's time for the Messiah to come.
JB	No, it's time for the revolution to come.
RV	Don't talk about that Bolshevik heresy in my house. We have to have faith.
JB	Bah. That's easy for you to say. The poor can't eat faith.
SH	Sha! Must you always argue?
LH	*more gentle* Jacob, you go back to Warsaw tomorrow. We may not see you for another year or more. Is this how you want us to remember you?
ZL	Maaa.
JB	*making peace* We don't have to argue. Aaron, can you tell me the story of you and Zlateh?
LM	Yes. How could a goat save your life?
AA	Well, it was just before Hanukkah last year – you remember how warm it was? It didn't feel like winter at all. The sun was shining and the grass was sprouting in the fields.
RV	Of course no one needed fur coats or caps. It was a very bad year. We had no money for the holidays, and I finally decided we had to sell Zlateh.

LH	She's old and doesn't give much milk. Twelve years isn't very old for a boy, but it's very old for a goat. Feyvel the butcher said he would give us eight gulden for her.
AA	Papa told me to take the goat to town. I knew what it meant, but I had to do what he said. I put on my quilted coat and my winter hat and toed a rope around Zlateh's neck. She stood there patiently and licked my hand.
CH	I cried.
LH	I gave him two slices of break with cheese to eat on the road. He was supposed to stay overnight with Feyvel and come home with the money the next day.
AA	When we went out on the road to Chelm, Zlateh seemed surprised. She'd never been led in that direction before. She looked at me and said –
ZL	Maaa.
AA	– and I knew it meant, "Where are you taking me?" But after a while she decided a goat shouldn't ask questions. We had never done her any harm. The sun was shining on the fields and pastures and thatched huts.

Sometimes dogs came running after us, but I chased them away with my stick.

RV Suddenly the weather changed. A big black cloud with a blueish center spread itself over the sky. A cold wind blew in with it. It started to hail, then to snow.

AA I never saw snow like that before. It snowed so hard the day got dark. Soon the road was covered and I didn't know where I was. Zlateh's legs were sinking into the snow. She said –

ZL Maaa.

AA – and it meant, "Why are we out in this storm?" I hoped someone would come by with a cart, but no one came.

Then the ground felt different. I realized we were in a plowed field. We had wandered off the road. I didn't know which way was Chelm, which way was Yanev. The wind whistles and howled. My hands and feet were numb, Zlateh had icicles in her beard. She stopped and planted her hooves and said –

ZL Maaa.

AA – "I can't go any farther. Can we go home now?"

RV — This wasn't just an ordinary storm. If Aaron didn't find shelter soon, he and Zlateh would freeze to death.

AA — Suddenly I saw something that looked like a hill. Why was there a hill in the middle of a field? I dragged Zlateh toward it. And I realized it was a haystack, covered with snow.

SH — Good thing Aaron's a village by and he knew what to do. He dug through the snow and hollowed out a nest inside the haystack for the goat and himself. Even in a blizzard, in the hay it is always warm.

AA — When Zlateh smelled the hay, she began to eat. She must have thought I was pretty clever to bring her to a whole house made out of food! I poked a kind of window through the hay with my stick so the air would come in.

JB — You must have been hungry after all that walking and digging.

AA — Yes. I ate my bread and cheese, but I was still hungry. Then I looked at Zlateh. Her udder was full of milk. So I lay down and milked her and squirted the milk in my mouth. It was rich and sweet.

LH

The snow kept falling for three days and two nights.

music

AA

Was it three days? It was dark most of the time. I didn't know if it was morning or night. the wind wailed with a thousand voices and whirled big plumes of snow. My window kept getting blocked with snow. Then the wind died down. It was so quiet my ears rang. I felt as if there had never been a summer – that snow was falling forever – that I never had a house or a family – Zlateh and I were snow children, born of snow.

We slept a lot of the time. I dreamed about green fields, blooming trees and singing birds. Zlateh ate the hay and I drank her milk. She kept me warm. I told her stories, and she always cocked her ears and listened. Then she said –

ZL

Maaa.

AA

– and I knew she meant, "We must be patient and accept whatever comes to us,"

I woke up and the snow had stopped. I dug my way out and looked at the world. It was all white, all quiet. It was night, and

I didn't want to try to go home in the dark. The sky cleared, and the moon was swimming in a sea of stars.

CH   Papa and the neighbors tried to search for Aaron and Zlateh during the storm. But there was no trace of them. We were terrified they were lost.

RV   On the morning after the storm, a villager was driving his sleigh down the road. Aaron heard the sleigh bells, and came out of the haystack. He could see the road now, and he led Zlateh, not to Feyvel the butcher, but home to us.

AA   *hugging Zlateh* I could never part with her. She saved my life. She's my best friend.

ZL   Maaa.

JB   A very limited language. But I think she's saying she loves you, too.

RV   The angels must have been watching over them.

LH   He's a very lucky boy.

JB   Hmph! I'd say she's a very lucky goat!

SH   Perhaps she has the soul of a departed saint.

JB   It's a good story, Aaron. You should write it down.

AA   Yes. I will.

RV   Yes. We need all our stories. We live today, but tomorrow what remains of it? Nothing more than a story. All of human life us one long story. The whole earth, all the stars and planets, represent one divine history, one source of life, one endless and wonderous story.

Music. Lights fade to just the menorah – then it fades, too.

*** END SCENE EIGHT***

END PLAY